TREATS

just great recipes

GENERAL INFORMATION

The level of difficulty of the recipes in this book
is expressed as a number from 1 (simple) to 3 (difficult).

TREATS

just great recipes

soups

MᶜRAE BOOKS

SERVES 4

PREPARATION 15 min

COOKING 25 min

DIFFICULTY level 1

Chicken Soup
with curry and corn

Heat 2 tablespoons of the oil in a large soup pot over medium-high heat. • Add the chicken and garlic and sauté until the chicken is cooked, 4–5 minutes. Remove the chicken and set aside. • Pour in the chicken stock and corn. Bring to a boil and simmer for 10 minutes. • Stir together the curry powder and rice wine in a small bowl until smooth. Stir into the simmering soup. Add the sugar and season with salt. Simmer for 5 more minutes. • In a small bowl, beat together the egg and remaining sesame oil. • Return the cooked chicken to the soup. Stir well and return to a gentle simmer. • Slowly pour the egg and sesame oil into the soup, stirring constantly. • Remove from the heat. Garnish with the scallions and serve hot.

3 tablespoons sesame oil

2 boneless, skinless chicken breasts (about 1 lb/500 g), cut into thin strips

2 cloves garlic, finely chopped

5 cups (1.25 liters) chicken stock (homemade or bouillon cube)

1 (14-oz/400-g) can corn (sweetcorn), drained

1 tablespoon curry powder

3 tablespoons rice wine

1 teaspoon sugar

Salt

1 large egg

2 tablespoons chopped scallions (green onions)

SERVES 6–8

PREPARATION 30 min

COOKING 1 h 30 m

DIFFICULTY level 1

Corn Chowder
with sweet potatoes

Sauté the bacon in a large soup pot over medium heat until brown, about 5 minutes. • Add the leeks, shallots, celery, and butter. Sauté gently for 5–10 minutes, reducing the heat if the leeks and shallots begin to brown. • Add the bay leaf, garlic, potatoes, sweet potatoes, and corn. Stir well. Cook for 5–10 minutes, stirring frequently. • Pour in the wine and sherry. Cook over medium heat until the liquid is reduced, 3–5 minutes. Add the parsley, thyme, salt, pepper, cayenne, and stock. Bring to a boil, then reduce heat to low. Partially cover and simmer until the potatoes are tender but still holding their shape, about 1 hour. • Stir in the cream. Sprinkle with the parsley and serve hot.

4 oz (100 g) bacon, diced

2 leeks, white and pale green part only, finely chopped

3 shallots, finely chopped

2 stalks celery, finely chopped

2 tablespoons butter

1 bay leaf

2 cloves garlic, finely chopped

3 medium potatoes, about 12 oz (350 g), peeled and cut small cubes

1 lb (500 g) sweet potatoes, peeled and cut into small cubes

2 cups (300 g) canned or frozen corn (sweetcorn)

1/3 cup (90 ml) dry white wine

3 tablespoons dry sherry

3 tablespoons finely chopped parsley + extra to garnish

1 tablespoon finely chopped thyme

1/2 teaspoon salt + more as needed

1 teaspoon freshly ground black pepper

1/4 teaspoon cayenne pepper

5 cups (1.25 liters) beef stock (homemade — see page 9 — or bouillon cube)

4 tablespoons heavy (double) cream

SERVES 6

PREPARATION 40 min + 12 h to soak

COOKING 3 h

DIFFICULTY level 1

Italian Soup
with garbanzo beans

Bring the water with the garbanzo beans to a boil in a large saucepan over medium-low heat. Skim off the froth. Cook over low heat for about 2 hours, or until the beans are very soft. • Season with salt and remove from the heat (there should still be plenty of cooking water). Drain, reserving the cooking water. • Cook the cardoons in salted boiling water until tender, 25–30 minutes. • Drain and set aside. • Sauté the mushrooms and sausage in the oil in a large saucepan over medium heat until the sausage is browned all over, about 10 minutes. • Sprinkle with the flour and season with salt and pepper. Pour in 6 cups (1.5 liters) of the reserved cooking water. Cover and simmer over medium heat for 30 minutes. • Stir in the cooked garbanzo beans and cardoons. • Add the pasta and cook until al dente, 5–7 minutes. • Serve hot.

- 4 quarts (4 liters) water, + more as required
- 2 cups (300 g) dried garbanzo beans (chickpeas), soaked overnight
- Salt
- 1 lb (500 g) cardoons or celery stalks, tough strings removed and coarsely chopped
- 1 oz (30 g) dried mushrooms, soaked in warm water for 15 minutes
- 2 Italian sausages, crumbled
- 1/3 cup (90 ml) extra-virgin olive oil
- 1 teaspoon all-purpose (plain) flour
- Freshly ground black pepper
- 12 oz (350 g) small dried soup pasta, such as ditalini

SERVES 4–6

PREPARATION 30 min

COOKING 40 min

DIFFICULTY level 2

Beef Stock
with semolina gnocchi

Bring the milk almost to a boil in a large deep saucepan. Whisk in the salt and semolina. • Bring to a boil and simmer over low heat for 15–20 minutes, stirring constantly with a wooden spoon. If it becomes gluey and difficult to stir, add the extra milk. • Pour into a large bowl and let cool, stirring occasionally. • Add the egg yolks, and butter and mix well. • Beat the egg whites in a separate bowl until frothy and add them to the mixture. • Shape into gnocchi about the size of marbles. • Bring the stock to a boil in a large saucepan. Cook the gnocchi in batches until they rise to the surface, 3–4 minutes. • Ladle the stock and gnocchi into serving bowls. Sprinkle with the Parmesan and serve hot.

4 cups (1 liter) milk, + more as needed (optional)

¼ teaspoon salt

1⅔ cups (250 g) semolina

2 large eggs, separated, + 2 large egg yolks

3 tablespoons butter, softened

6 cups (1.5 liters) beef stock (see recipe opposite)

1 cup (125 g) freshly grated Parmesan

SERVES 4

PREPARATION 40 min + 1 h to rest

COOKING 3 h 30 min

DIFFICULTY level 2

Beef Stock

with rye bread gnocchi

Beef Stock: Stick the cloves into the onion quarters. • Place all the ingredients in a large soup pot and cover with the water. Bring the mixture to a boil over medium-low heat. • Simmer over low heat for 3 hours. Skim the stock during cooking to remove the scum that will rise to the surface. • Strain the stock, discarding the vegetables. Gnocchi: Place the bread in a large bowl and mix in the pancetta, onion, leek, and garlic. • Mix the milk, water, and salt in a small bowl. • Pour the milk over the bread mixture and let rest for 1 hour. • Use your hands to knead in the cornmeal. • Form the mixture into balls the size of walnuts and dust lightly with flour. • Bring the stock to a boil in a large saucepan. Add the dumplings and simmer until cooked through, about 20 minutes. • Ladle into bowls and serve hot.

Beef Stock
4 whole cloves (optional)
1 large onion, cut into quarters
1 large carrot, cut in half
1 leek
2 stalks celery, including leaves
Small bunch parsley
2 bay leaves
2 cloves garlic, peeled
2 very ripe tomatoes
1 tablespoon coarse sea salt
2 lb (1 kg) boiling beef
2 lb (1 kg) beef bones
About 4 quarts (4 liters) cold water

Gnocchi
10 oz (300 g) rye bread, crusts removed
1 1/3 cups (180 g) finely chopped smoked pancetta or bacon
1 small red onion, finely chopped
1 large leek, white part only, finely chopped
1 clove garlic, finely chopped
3 tablespoons milk
3 tablespoons water
Salt
1/3 cup (30 g) fine polenta (stoneground cornmeal)
1/3 cup (30 g) all-purpose (plain) flour

SERVES 4–6

PREPARATION 1 h + 12 h to soak

COOKING 3 h

DIFFICULTY level 1

Minestrone

with lentils and beans

Bring 8 cups (2 liters) of water to a boil in a large saucepan with the garbanzo beans and lentils. Skim off any foam. Reduce the heat and simmer until the beans are almost tender, about 1 hour. • Drain, reserving the stock. • Sauté the pancetta in the oil in a large saucepan over low heat for 5 minutes. • Add the onion and sauté for 5 more minutes. • Add the herbs and tomatoes and cook for 3 minutes. • Add the remaining 8 cups (2 liters) of water and the ham bone, if using, and bring to a boil. Season with salt and add all the vegetables. • Simmer over medium-low heat for 30 minutes. • Add the drained beans and lentils and about half of the reserved stock. Chop the garlic and lard and add to the pot. • Cook until the vegetables are tender, 30–45 minutes. • Cook the pasta in the boiling soup until al dente. If there is not enough liquid, add more of the reserved stock as needed. • Sprinkle with Pecorino and season with black pepper. Serve hot.

4 quarts (4 liters) water

1 cup (150 g) dried garbanzo beans (chickpeas), soaked overnight

1 cup (150 g) lentils

1/2 cup (60 g) finely chopped pancetta

1/4 cup (60 ml) extra-virgin olive oil

1 onion, finely chopped

3 tablespoons finely chopped mixed fresh herbs (such as marjoram, thyme, parsley, and sage)

1 cup (250 ml) tomato passata (sieved tomatoes)

1 ham bone (optional)

Salt

1 lb (500 g) mixed vegetables (carrots, celery, spinach, Swiss chard, potatoes, zucchini/courgettes, finely chopped

2 cloves garlic

1/4 cup (30 g) lard or butter, cut up

8 oz (250 g) ditalini pasta

1/4 cup (30 g) freshly grated Pecorino

Freshly ground black pepper

SERVES 4

PREPARATION 15 min

COOKING 30 min

DIFFICULTY level 1

Beef Soup

with chilies and tamarind

Bring the stock to a boil in a large soup pot over medium heat. Add the potatoes, carrots, water chestnuts, broccoli, soy sauce, tamarind, and beef. Cover and simmer over low heat for 20 minutes, stirring occasionally. • Add the mushrooms and cook for 5 minutes. Add the bean sprouts, scallions, and chile peppers. Cook for 5 minutes more. • Season with salt and pepper. Serve hot.

6 cups (1.5 liters) beef stock (see page 9)

6 new potatoes, halved

6 carrots, cut into thin lengths

1 cup (100 g) chopped water chestnuts

4 oz (125 g) broccoli, chopped

3 tablespoons dark soy sauce

2 tablespoons tamarind paste

12 oz (350 g) beef filet, cut into strips

6 oz (180 g) shiitake mushrooms, thinly sliced

4 oz (125 g) mung bean sprouts

4 scallions (green onions), white and tender green parts only, chopped

2 fresh green chile peppers, seeded and finely chopped

2 fresh red chile peppers, seeded and finely chopped

Salt and freshly ground black pepper

SERVES 6–8

PREPARATION 20 min

COOKING 50 min

DIFFICULTY level 2

Chicken Soup
with lentils and lime

Heat the oil in a large soup pot over medium heat. Add the onion, celery, and carrot and sauté until softened, 7–10 minutes. • Stir in the garlic, thyme, and cumin. Add the lentils, stock, lime zest, and bay leaf, and bring to a boil. Cover and simmer until the lentils are softened, 30–40 minutes. • Discard the bay leaf and add 1 tablespoon of the lime juice. • Remove from the heat and let cool slightly. • Blend with a handheld blender until smooth. Return the pan to the heat and reheat gently. If the soup is too thick, add a little water. Season with salt and pepper and add more lime juice to taste. • Garnish with the parsley and serve hot.

3 tablespoons extra-virgin olive oil
1 large onion, finely chopped
1 stalk celery, finely chopped
1 carrot, finely chopped
1 clove garlic, finely chopped
1 tablespoon finely chopped thyme
$1/2$ teaspoon cumin seeds
$1\frac{2}{3}$ cups (350 g) red lentils
8 cups (2 liters) chicken stock
Grated zest of $1/4$ lime
1 bay leaf
2 tablespoons fresh lime juice
Salt and freshly ground black pepper
2 tablespoons finely chopped parsley

SERVES 4–6

PREPARATION 40 min

COOKING 1 h 15 min

DIFFICULTY level 1

Spelt Soup

Place the ham bone in a large saucepan and pour in the water. Add the onion, carrot, celery, tomato, parsley, and peppercorns. Bring to a boil over low heat and simmer until all the vegetables are very tender, about 45 minutes. • Use a slotted spoon to remove the vegetables and process them in a food processor or blender until smooth. • Remove the meat from the bone and return the meat to the saucepan. Add the puréed vegetables. Season with salt and bring to a boil. • Add the spelt and cook, stirring occasionally, until the spelt is tender, about 30 minutes. • Sprinkle with Pecorino and serve hot.

1 raw salted ham bone (with some ham still on the bone)
2 quarts (2 liters) water
1 onion, cut into quarters
1 carrot, coarsely chopped
1 stalk celery, coarsely chopped
1 firm-ripe tomato, cut in half
4 sprigs fresh parsley
1/4 teaspoon whole black peppercorns
Salt
2 cups (200 g) crushed spelt (farro)
3/4 cup (90 g) freshly grated Pecorino cheese

Endive Soup

SERVES 4

PREPARATION 20 min

COOKING 20 min

DIFFICULTY level 1

Cook the Belgian endive in a large saucepan of salted boiling water until tender, about 10 minutes. • Drain and chop in a food processor until smooth. • Transfer to a large bowl and mix in the eggs, Parmesan, and nutmeg. • Pour the boiling stock over the egg mixture and mix well. • Arrange the bread in individual serving bowls and ladle the soup over the top. • Serve hot.

14 oz (400 g) Belgian endive or Swiss chard (silver beet), rinsed and finely shredded

4 eggs, lightly beaten

4 tablespoons freshly grated Parmesan

$1/8$ teaspoon freshly grated nutmeg

5 cups (1.25 liters) beef stock (see page 9), boiling

4 slices firm-textured bread, toasted

Tortellini
in beef stock

Pasta: Sift the flour and salt into a medium bowl. Break the eggs in and mix to make a smooth dough. Knead until smooth and elastic, 15–20 minutes. Shape into a ball, wrap in plastic wrap (cling film), and let rest for 30 minutes. • Filling: Heat the butter and sage in a small saucepan over medium heat. Add the pork and sauté until browned. • Add the chicken liver and sauté for 2–3 minutes. • Add the mortadella and sauté for 3 minutes. • Remove from the heat and discard the sage. • Chop finely in a food processor. Transfer to a large bowl and mix in the egg, Parmesan, salt, pepper, and nutmeg. • Roll out the dough on a lightly floured surface until very thin. Cut into 1$\frac{1}{2}$-inch (4-cm) squares and drop a nugget of filling the size of walnuts into the centers. • Fold into tortellini. • Cook the pasta in the boiling stock for 3–5 minutes. • Serve hot with the Parmesan.

Pasta
2 cups (300 g) all-purpose (plain) flour
$\frac{1}{4}$ teaspoon salt
3 large eggs

Filling
2 tablespoons butter
5 leaves fresh sage
12 oz (300 g) pork loin, cut into small
    chunks
1 chicken liver, trimmed and cut into
    quarters
1$\frac{1}{4}$ cups (150 g) diced mortadella
1 large egg
$\frac{1}{4}$ cup (30 g) freshly grated Parmesan
    cheese
Salt and freshly ground black pepper
$\frac{1}{8}$ teaspoon freshly grated nutmeg

To Serve
8 cups (2 liters) beef stock (homemade
    – see page 9 – or bouillon cube),
    boiling
$\frac{3}{4}$ cup (90 g) freshly grated Parmesan
    cheese

If preferred, use storebought tortellini
    and serve in the boiling beef stock

SERVES 4–6

PREPARATION 30 min

COOKING 30 min + min for fresh clams

DIFFICULTY level 2

Clam Chowder

Wash the fresh clams and place in a large soup pot with the water and 1 teaspoon of the butter. Simmer until the clams have opened up, 8–10 minutes. • Strain the clams through a large strainer into a large bowl. Reserve the stock. Discard any unopened shells. Remove the meat from the rest. • Chop the larger clams and leave the small ones whole. • If you are using canned clams, drain the juices and add to the water or clam juice. • If you are using frozen clams, defrost them first. • Melt the remaining butter in the same soup pot over medium heat. Add the onion, celery, and garlic and $1/2$ teaspoon salt and sauté over medium heat until softened, about 5 minutes. • Mix in the flour and stir in the clam stock (or fish stock) and the wine. Add the potatoes, bay leaf, and allspice. Simmer until the potatoes are tender, about 10 minutes. • Add the corn and cook for 5 more minutes. • Remove from the heat and discard the bay leaf and allspice berries. Stir in the cream and clams. Cook for 3 minutes more, but do not bring to a boil. Season with salt and pepper to taste. • Serve hot.

3 lb (1.5 kg) fresh clams (about 30 clams) or 1 (10-oz/300-g) can or 12 oz (350 g) frozen clam meat

$1^{1}/_{4}$ cups (310 ml) water or bottled clam juice, if using canned clams

1 teaspoon + $^{1}/_{4}$ cup (60 g) butter

1 onion, finely chopped

1 stalk celery, finely chopped

2 cloves garlic, finely chopped

Salt

2 tablespoons all-purpose (plain) flour

$^{2}/_{3}$ cup (150 ml) dry white wine

3 medium potatoes, diced

1 bay leaf

2 allspice berries

1 cup (100 g) frozen corn kernels or kernels from 1 ear fresh corn

$1^{1}/_{2}$ cups (375 ml) heavy (double) cream

Freshly ground black pepper

Beef Stock

with bread dumplings

Soak the bread in the milk for 10 minutes, or until softened. Drain, squeezing out the excess milk. • Sauté the onion in 2 tablespoons of butter in a small frying pan over low heat for 20 minutes, until very soft and golden. • Season with salt, remove from the heat, and let cool. • Use a wooden spoon to beat the remaining butter in a large bowl until softened. • Add the soaked bread to the butter with the sautéed onion, flour, 1 tablespoon of the parsley, eggs, and nutmeg. • Form the mixture into walnut-sized dumplings. • Simmer the dumplings in a large pot with the stock until cooked, about 7 minutes. • Sprinkle with the remaining parsley and serve hot.

1 lb (500 g) day-old bread, crusts removed and crumbled

1¼ cups (310 ml) milk

1 onion, finely chopped

⅓ cup (90 g) butter

Salt

¾ cup (125 g) all-purpose (plain) flour

1 small bunch parsley, finely chopped

5 large eggs

⅛ teaspoon freshly grated nutmeg

4 cups (1 liter) beef stock (see page 9), boiling

SERVES 6

PREPARATION 1 h + 1 h to dry pasta

COOKING 15 min

DIFFICULTY level 2

Beef Stock
with fresh pasta

Pasta Dough: Sift the flour, salt, and nutmeg onto a work surface and make a well in the center. Break the eggs into the well and use a fork to mix in. Stir in the Parmesan to make a smooth dough. • Knead for 15–20 minutes, until smooth and elastic. Shape the dough into a ball, wrap in plastic wrap (cling film), and let rest for 10 minutes. • Divide the dough into four and roll out to a thickness of about ¾ inch (2 cm). Let dry on a kitchen cloth for 10 minutes. • Cut the slices finely until the pasta resembles grains of rice. • Spread out on a clean surface and let dry for at least 1 hour in a dry, airy place. • Bring the stock to a boil and cook the pasta until al dente, 1–2 minutes. Sprinkle with Parmesan and serve hot.

Pasta Dough
2⅔ cups (400 g) all-purpose (plain) flour
¼ teaspoon salt
⅛ teaspoon freshly grated nutmeg
3 tablespoons freshly grated Parmesan
4 large eggs

To Serve
2 quarts (2 liters) beef stock (see page 9)
¾ cup (90 g) freshly grated Parmesan

SERVES 6–8

PREPARATION 25 min

COOKING 35 min

DIFFICULTY level 2

Corn Chowder

with potatoes and bell peppers

Heat the oil in a large soup pot over medium heat. Add the onions, garlic, chile, celery, and carrot and sauté until softened, about 5 minutes. • Add the salt. Cover and cook until the vegetables are tender, 5–10 minutes. • Add the cornstarch mixture and stir until blended. • Add the potatoes and corn. • Dissolve the tomato paste in 4 cups (1 liter) of the stock. Whisk the mixture into the vegetables. • Bring to a boil and simmer until the potatoes are just tender but not mushy, 8–10 minutes. • Add the bell peppers and pour in the remaining 4 cups (1 liter) of stock. Return to a gentle boil. Stir in the basil, parsley, and cream, if using, and serve hot.

3 tablespoons extra-virgin olive oil
2 small onions, finely chopped
2 cloves garlic, finely chopped
1 mild red or green chile pepper, seeded and finely chopped
1 stalk celery, thinly sliced
1 carrot, thinly sliced
1 teaspoon salt
1 tablespoon cornstarch (cornflour), dissolved in $1/4$ cup (60 ml) water
1 lb (500 g) small new potatoes, thinly sliced
1 lb (500 g) frozen corn (sweet corn)
1 teaspoon tomato paste (concentrate)
8 cups (2 liters) chicken stock (homemade or bouillon cube)
2 red bell peppers (capsicums), seeded and diced
2 tablespoons finely chopped fresh basil
1 tablespoon finely chopped parsley
$1/3$ cup (90 ml) heavy (double) cream (optional)

SERVES 4–6

PREPARATION 20 min

COOKING 30 min

DIFFICULTY level 2

Bourride

Place the leeks, shallot, and potatoes in layers in a large saucepan with the garlic (if using). Lay the pieces of fish on top and pour in the stock and wine. Poach gently (do not boil) until the fish is just cooked, 10–15 minutes. • Use a slotted spoon to transfer the fish to a serving dish and keep warm. • Bring the cooking liquid to a boil and simmer over high heat until reduced to half of its original volume. • Remove the potatoes when tender and keep warm. • Warm 1¼ cups (310 ml) of the aïoli in a saucepan over low heat. Strain the reduced stock and gradually pour it into the aïoli, whisking constantly. Bring the soup to a simmer. Do not boil. It should be thick, pale, and creamy. Season with salt and pepper. • Place a slice of toast in individual soup bowls and arrange the fish and potato on top. Ladle the soup over the top. • Garnish with the remaining aïoli, if liked, and sprinkle with the parsley. • Serve hot.

To prepare the aïoli: crush the garlic using a mortar and pestle or garlic crusher. Place in a medium bowl and stir in the egg yolks and vinegar. • Add the oil in a thin steady trickle (as you would if making mayonnaise), stirring constantly, until smooth and creamy. season with salt.

2 leeks, white part only, thinly sliced
1 shallot, finely sliced
1 lb (500 g) potatoes, peeled and thinly sliced
2 cloves garlic, crushed (optional)
2 lb (1 kg) firm-textured white fish fillets, such as cod, brill, turbot, or monkfish
4 cups (1 liter) fish stock
⅔ cup (150 ml) dry white wine
1 quantity aïoli (see below)
Salt and freshly ground black pepper
4–6 slices French bread, toasted
2 tablespoons finely chopped flat-leaf parsley, to garnish

Aïoli
6 cloves garlic
2 large egg yolks
1 tablespoon white wine vinegar
2 cups (500 ml) extra-virgin olive oil
Salt

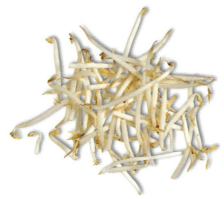

SERVES 4–6

PREPARATION 30 min

COOKING 30 min

DIFFICULTY level 2

Chicken
noodle soup

Mix the tamarind, chile oil, chilies, garlic, ginger, and soy and oyster sauces in a large wok. Warm the wok over medium heat. • Add the sugar and curry leaves, if using, and pour in the stock. Bring to a boil, stirring constantly. Simmer for 5 minutes. • Add the chicken and simmer for another 5 minutes, stirring often. • Stir in the carrots, sprouts, baby corn, bell peppers, and rice noodles and simmer until the chicken and vegetables are tender, about 10 minutes. • Season with salt. Garnish with the cilantro and serve hot.

2 tablespoons tamarind paste

1 tablespoon Asian chile oil

5 dried red chilies, pounded well

5 cloves garlic, finely chopped

1 tablespoon minced fresh ginger

1/4 cup (60 ml) dark soy sauce

1 tablespoon oyster sauce

1 tablespoon sugar

6 curry leaves (optional)

6 cups (1.5 liters) chicken stock (homemade or bouillon cube)

2 boneless, skinless chicken breasts, cut into thin strips

2 medium carrots, finely chopped

1 cup (125 g) bean sprouts

6–8 baby corn (sweetcorn)

1/2 cup (125 g) chopped green bell peppers (capsicums)

4 oz (125 g) chopped red bell peppers (capsicums)

6 oz (180 g) rice vermicelli

Salt

2 tablespoons chopped cilantro (coriander), to garnish

Butternut Squash
Soup

Melt the butter in a large saucepan over medium heat. Add the onions, garlic, salt, cumin, coriander, and mustard and sauté until the onions are tender, about 5 minutes. • Add the squash, potato, honey, chile, and ginger. Pour in 4 cups (1 liter) of the stock and bring to a boil over low heat. Cover and simmer until the vegetables have softened, about 15 minutes. • Add the beans, remaining 2 cups (500 ml) of stock, and half the lemon juice. Simmer for 5 minutes. Remove from the heat and let cool slightly. • Blend with a handheld blender until smooth. Return the pan to the heat and reheat gently, adding the remaining lemon juice and more stock if needed. Season with salt, pepper, and cayenne. • Swirl in the yogurt and garnish with the red bell pepper. Serve hot.

2 tablespoons butter

2 small onions, finely chopped

1 clove garlic, finely chopped

1 teaspoon salt

$1/2$ teaspoon ground cumin

$1/2$ teaspoon ground coriander seeds

$1/2$ teaspoon dry mustard powder

2 medium butternut squash, peeled, seeded, and cut into small cubes

1 sweet potato or white potato, cubed

1 teaspoon honey

1 green chile pepper, finely chopped

1-inch (2.5-cm) piece fresh ginger, peeled and finely chopped

6 cups (1.5 liters) chicken stock

2 cups (400 g) canned garbanzo beans (chickpeas)

Juice of 2 lemons

Salt and freshly ground black pepper

$1/2$ teaspoon cayenne pepper

$1/2$ cup (125 ml) plain yogurt

2 tablespoons diced red bell pepper (capsicum)

Corn Soup
with chicken and chile

Heat the oil in a medium saucepan over high heat. Add the chicken and sauté until white, 7–8 minutes. Set aside. • Pour the milk into the pan and add the onion and potatoes. Bring to a boil. Lower the heat and add the cilantro, chilies, and half the corn. Simmer over very low heat for 10 minutes, stirring often. Remove from the heat. • Blend with a handheld blender until smooth. Mix in the cornstarch paste. • Return the soup to the heat and reheat gently until thickened. Bring to a boil again and add the remaining corn. Simmer until the corn is cooked, about 3 minutes. • Remove from the heat and season with salt and pepper. Stir in the cream and keep stirring for 3 minutes. Stir in the chives and chicken. Serve hot.

1 boneless, skinless chicken breast, cut into small pieces

1 tablespoon extra-virgin olive oil

4 cups (1 liter) milk

1 large onion, finely chopped

12 oz (350 g) potatoes, peeled and diced

2 tablespoons finely chopped fresh cilantro (coriander)

3 fresh red bird's eye chile peppers, seeded and finely chopped

1 lb (500 g) frozen or canned corn (sweet corn)

1 tablespoon cornstarch (cornflour) mixed with 3 tablespoons cold water

Salt and freshly ground black pepper

3 tablespoons snipped chives

$^{1}/_{2}$ cup (125 ml) light (single) cream

3 tablespoons snipped fresh chives

Goulash Soup

Melt the butter in a large soup pot over high heat. Add the beef in batches and cook until seared, 1–2 minutes. Set the seared meat aside. • Add the onions and sauté for until softened, about 5 minutes. • Add the garlic, thyme, and caraway seeds and sauté for 2 minutes more. • Add the paprika and ½ teaspoon of salt. Sauté over medium heat until all the paprika has been incorporated, about 5 minutes. • Sprinkle in the flour and mix well. • Pour in 1 cup (250 ml) of the stock. Simmer over low heat for 1 minute, stirring constantly. • Stir in the tomato paste, bell pepper, and tomatoes and pour in the remaining 7 cups (1.75 liters) of stock. Return the meat to the pan. Bring to a boil. Cover and simmer over low heat until the meat is tender, about 1½ hours. Add more stock if the soup begins to thicken in the early stages of the cooking time. • Stir in the cream and wine and cook for 1 minute. Season with salt and pepper to taste. • Serve the soup hot with the sour cream passed on the side.

¼ cup (60 g) butter

1½ lb (750 g) lean beef (stew beef), cut into small chunks

3 medium onions, finely chopped

3 cloves garlic, finely chopped

1 teaspoon dried thyme

½ teaspoon caraway seeds, crushed

2 tablespoons hot paprika

Salt

1½ tablespoons all-purpose (plain) flour

8 cups (2 liters) beef stock + more as needed (homemade — see page 9 — o bouillon cube)

1 tablespoon tomato paste (concentrate)

1 green bell pepper (capsicum), seeded and thinly sliced

3 ripe tomatoes, peeled and quartered

¼ cup (60 ml) light (single) cream

¼ cup (60 ml) dry red wine

Freshly ground black pepper

½ cup (125 ml) sour cream, to serve

Tomato Soup
with noodles

Heat the oil over medium-high in a large saucepan. Add the onion, garlic, and cumin, if using, and sauté until the onion is softened, about 5 minutes. • Add the tomatoes and 2 cups (500 ml) of the stock. Reduce the heat to low, partially cover the pot, and simmer for 30 minutes. • Add the remaining chicken stock and the soaked noodles. Raise the heat to medium and bring to a boil. • Remove from the heat, garnish with the basil, if using, and serve hot.

2 tablespoons extra-virgin olive oil

1 large white onion, finely chopped

4 cloves garlic, finely chopped

1/2 teaspoon cumin seeds, freshly ground (optional)

2 (14-oz/400-g) cans tomatoes, chopped, with juice

3 cups (750 ml) chicken stock (homemade or bouillon cube)

Salt and freshly ground white pepper

4 (3-oz/90-g) packages ramen noodles (350 g instant noodles), flavor packet discarded, soaked in boiling water for 10 minutes (or according to instructions on the package)

1–2 tablespoons finely chopped basil, to garnish (optional)

Soup
with beans and herbs

Heat the oil in a large saucepan over medium heat. Add the onion, carrot, and celery and sauté until softened, 7–10 minutes. • Stir in the beans, parsley stems, sage, garlic, tomatoes, and stock. Season with pepper. Bring to a boil and add the rosemary. Simmer over very low heat until the beans are tender but not mushy, 60–90 minutes. • Discard the rosemary. Add the green beans and basil. Simmer until the green beans are tender but still crunchy, for 5–7 minutes. • Season with salt and pepper to taste. Stir in the celery leaves. • Garnish with parsley leaves and drizzle with oil. Serve hot.

1/3 cup (90 ml) extra-virgin olive oil + extra to drizzle

1 onion, finely chopped

1 carrot, finely chopped

1 stalk celery, finely chopped

2 cups (250 g) dried cannellini, white kidney, or borlotti beans, soaked overnight and drained

Handful of parsley stems, finely chopped

3 leaves fresh sage, finely chopped

2 cloves garlic, finely chopped

5 ripe cherry tomatoes

8 cups (2 liters) vegetable stock (homemade or bouillon cube)

Salt and freshly ground black pepper

2 sprigs fresh rosemary

5 oz (150 g) green beans or snow peas (mangetout), trimmed and chopped

Handful of fresh basil

Salt

Handful of celery leaves

1 tablespoon coarsely chopped parsley

SERVES 6

PREPARATION 10 min

COOKING 40 min

DIFFICULTY level 1

Leek and Potato
soup with rye bread

Melt the butter in a large saucepan over medium heat. Add the garlic, celery, leeks, and potatoes. Sauté until softened, about 10 minutes. • Add the stock and bring to a boil. Simmer over low heat until the vegetables are all very tender, about 30 minutes. • Toast the bread until lightly browned all over. • Place a piece of toast in each of 6 soup bowls. Cover each piece with a slice or two of cheese and a spoonful of the cooked vegetables. Add another piece of toast and some of the remaining cheese. Ladle the soup over the top. • Let the bowls of soup rest for 2 minutes. Season with pepper and serve hot.

1 tablespoon butter

1 clove garlic, finely chopped

2 celery sticks, finely chopped

2 small leeks, finely sliced

1 lb (500 g) waxy potatoes, peeled and cut into small cubes

8 cups (2 liters) vegetable stock (homemade or bouillon cube)

6 thick slices of rye bread, cut in half

10 oz (300 g) Fontina or other mild cheese, thinly sliced

Freshly ground black pepper

SERVES 4–6

PREPARATION 10 min

COOKING 30 min

DIFFICULTY level 1

Pasta Soup
with vegetables and pesto

Pesto: Purée the basil, pine nuts, and garlic in a food processor until smooth. • Add the cheese and oil and mix well. • Soup: Bring the stock to a boil in a large saucepan over medium heat. Add the green beans and potatoes. Season with salt and pepper and simmer for 15 minutes. • Add the pasta and cook until al dente and the vegetables are very tender, 5–7 minutes. • Add the pesto and mix well. Ladle into serving bowls. Serve hot.

Pesto
2 oz (60 g) basil leaves
1/4 cup (45 g) pine kernels
2 cloves garlic
1/2 cup (60 g) freshly grated Parmesan
1/3 cup (90 ml) extra-virgin olive oil

Soup
8 cups (2 liters) vegetable stock
   (homemade or bouillon cube)
12 oz (350 g) green beans,
   cut in short lengths
2 large waxy (boiling) potatoes, peeled
   and cut into small cubes
Salt and freshly ground black pepper
8 oz (250 g) farfalline or other small
   soup pasta

SERVES 4

PREPARATION 20 min

COOKING 35 min

DIFFICULTY level 1

Kasha Soup
with wild mushrooms

Heat the oil in a large saucepan over medium heat. Add the onion and sauté until softened, about 5 minutes. • Stir in the mushrooms and garlic. Sauté until the mushrooms have softened slightly, about 5 minutes. • Add the kasha and bay leaf. Pour in the water. • Bring to a boil, lower the heat, and simmer until the kasha is tender and the mushrooms are cooked, about 20 minutes. • Season with salt and pepper. Swirl in the sour cream and garnish with the thyme. Remove the bay leaf. • Serve hot.

1/4 cup (60 ml) extra-virgin olive oil
1 medium onion, finely chopped
6 oz (180 g) mixed wild mushrooms, thinly sliced
2 cloves garlic, finely chopped
4 oz (125 g) kasha (buckwheat groats)
1 bay leaf
4 cups (1 liter) water
Salt and freshly ground black pepper
1/4 cup (60 ml) sour cream, to garnish
1 tablespoon finely chopped thyme, to garnish

Bean Soup
with pesto

Heat the oil in a large saucepan over medium heat. Add the onion and sauté until softened, about 5 minutes. • Add the butter beans, potatoes, and stock and bring to a boil. • Simmer over low heat for 20 minutes, or until the beans and potatoes are tender. Stir in the pesto. • Remove the pan from the heat and blend with a handheld blender until smooth. • Return the pan to the heat and reheat gently. Season with salt and pepper and garnish with the basil.

2 tablespoons extra-virgin olive oil

1 onion, finely chopped

14 oz (400 g) frozen butter beans or lima beans

8 oz (250 g) potatoes, peeled and cut into small cubes

4 cups (1 liter) vegetable or chicken stock (homemade or bouillon cube)

1 quantity pesto (see page 37)

Salt and freshly ground black pepper

1 tablespoon torn basil

SERVES 4–6

PREPARATION 30 min

COOKING 40 min

DIFFICULTY level 2

Bread Soup
with tomato and bell peppers

Preheat the broiler (grill) on a high setting. Grill the bell peppers, turning them from time to time, until they are charred all over. Remove from the grill and transfer to a plastic bag. Seal the bag and let rest for 10 minutes. Remove the peppers from the bag. Peel them, then discard the seeds. Slice the peppers finely. • Heat the oil in a large saucepan over medium heat. Add the garlic and sauté until pale golden brown, 2–3 minutes. • Add the tomatoes and half the bell peppers. Bring to a boil. • Add the bread and mix well. Add the stock and mix well. Season with black pepper and bring to a boil. Simmer until the bread has broken down, about 15 minutes. Season with salt and add the basil and marjoram. • Ladle into serving bowls and top with the remaining peppers. Garnish with the basil. Serve hot or at room temperature.

3 large red bell peppers (capsicums)

$1/4$ cup (60 ml) extra-virgin olive oil

2 cloves garlic, finely chopped

$1\frac{1}{2}$ lb (750 g) ripe tomatoes, chopped

8 oz (250 g) crusty white bread, preferably unsalted

3 cups (750 ml) vegetable stock (homemade or bouillon cube)

Salt and freshly ground black pepper

2 tablespoons finely chopped basil, + extra leaves, to garnish

2 tablespoons finely chopped marjoram

Fennel Miso

Heat the oil in a large soup pot over medium heat. Add the fennel, carrot, leeks, and potatoes and sauté until the vegetables are softened, 8–10 minutes. • Stir in the ginger, garlic, chilies, and fennel seeds. Season with salt and sauté over low heat for 10 minutes more. • Dissolve the miso in $\frac{1}{2}$ cup (125 ml) of the boiling water. • Stir the miso mixture and remaining water into the soup. Simmer until the potatoes are tender, 15–20 minutes. • Add the watercress, snowpeas, and lemon juice. Simmer for 3 minutes more. • Garnish with the parsley and reserved watercress leaves. Serve hot.

2 tablespoons extra-virgin olive oil

1 lb (500 g) fennel bulbs, cut into wedges and finely sliced

1 carrot, cut into very thin strips

Whites of 2 leeks, trimmed and sliced

2 potatoes, peeled and cut into small cubes

1-inch (2.5-cm) piece fresh ginger, peeled and finely chopped

1 clove garlic, finely chopped

$\frac{1}{2}$ green chile pepper, finely chopped

1 red chile pepper, finely chopped

1 teaspoon fennel seeds

Salt

6 cups (1.5 liters) water, boiling

3 tablespoons barley miso

4 oz (125 g) watercress, stems coarsely chopped, + extra leaves to garnish

5 snowpeas (mangetout), chopped

1 tablespoon fresh lemon juice

1 tablespoon finely chopped parsley

SERVES 4

PREPARATION 20 min

COOKING 25 min

DIFFICULTY level I

Broccoli Soup
with cheese toasts

Separate the broccoli into florets. Chop the stalk into small dice and coarsely chop the leaves. • Heat 2 tablespoons of the oil in a large saucepan over high heat. Add the garlic and sauté until soft, 2–3 minutes. • Add the broccoli, (leaves, florets, and stalks), potato, and stock. Season with salt and pepper. Partially cover and cook over low heat until the broccoli is tender, about 15 minutes. • Remove from the heat and chop in a food processor until smooth. Ladle the soup into soup bowls. • Sprinkle the toasted bread with cheese and bell pepper. Garnish the soup with the toast.

I large head broccoli (about 2 lb/I kg)
¼ cup (60 ml) extra-virgin olive oil
2–3 cloves garlic, finely chopped
I large potato, peeled and diced
6 cups (1.5 liters) chicken stock
   (homemade or bouillon cube)
Salt and freshly ground white pepper
4–6 slices bread, cut in half, toasted
½ cup (60 g) freshly grated Cheddar
   or Emmenthal cheese
I–2 tablespoons diced red bell pepper
   (capsicum)

SERVES 4

PREPARATION 15 min

COOKING 40 min

DIFFICULTY level 1

Garlic Soup

Place the water and garlic in a large saucepan over medium heat. Add the cloves and sage and season with salt and pepper. Bring to a boil. Simmer until the garlic is very tender, about 20 minutes. • Preheat the oven to 400°F (200°C/gas 6). • Arrange the slices of baguette on an oiled baking sheet. Top each piece of bread with a little of the cheese. Drizzle with the oil and season with pepper. Bake until crisp and lightly browned, 5–7 minutes. • Purée the soup in a blender until smooth and creamy. • Arrange the crostini in serving bowls and then ladle the soup over the top. • Serve hot.

6 cups (1.5 liters) water
30 cloves garlic, peeled
2 cloves
3 sage leaves
Salt and freshly ground black pepper
1 large baguette (French loaf), sliced
6 oz (180 g) Gruyère, coarsely grated
1/4 cup (60 ml) extra-virgin olive oil

Red Lentil Soup
with mango

Place the lentils in a large pot of cold water and bring to a boil. Simmer until tender, 30–35 minutes. Drain and set aside. • Heat the oil over low heat in the same pot. Add the onion, garlic, and mango and sauté until softened, about 5 minutes. • Add the lentils and potatoes and pour in the stock. Bring to a boil and simmer over low heat for 30 minutes. • Stir in the tomatoes, cumin, chile, paprika, and thyme. Season with salt and pepper. Simmer for 10 minutes. • Stir in the lemon juice. Remove from the heat and blend with a handheld blender until partially smooth. • Return to the heat and reheat gently. Serve hot with the toast.

1 cup (100 g) red lentils, rinsed
1 tablespoon extra-virgin olive oil
1/2 onion, finely sliced
2 cloves garlic, finely chopped
3 tablespoons chopped dried mango
2 potatoes, peeled and diced
3 cups (750 ml) chicken stock (homemade or bouillon cube)
1 (14-oz/400-g) can tomatoes, with juice
1/2 teaspoon ground cumin
1/2 teaspoon ground red chile
1/2 teaspoon sweet paprika
1/2 teaspoon dried thyme
Salt and freshly ground black pepper
2 tablespoons fresh lemon juice
Warm toasted, buttered, to serve

Black-Eyed Pea
soup with cilantro

Heat the oil in the oil in a large saucepan over medium heat. Add the shallots, celery, garlic, and chile pepper, and sauté until softened, about 7 minutes. • Pour in the stock and add the beans. Bring to a boil. Cover and simmer over low heat, until the peas are almost soft, 40–50 minutes. • Add the cayenne and season with salt and pepper. Add the tomatoes and simmer until tender, 20 minutes. • Stir in the lime juice and 1 tablespoon of cilantro. Garnish with the remaining cilantro and serve hot.

2 tablespoons extra-virgin olive oil

4 shallots, finely chopped

4 stalks celery, coarsely chopped

4 cloves garlic, finely chopped

1 fresh red or green chile, seeded and finely chopped

8 cups (2 liters) chicken stock (homemade or bouillon cube)

1½ cups (150 g) black-eyed peas, soaked overnight and drained

¼ teaspoon cayenne pepper

Salt and freshly ground black pepper

5 tomatoes, peeled and chopped

Juice of 2 limes

2 tablespoons finely chopped cilantro (coriander)

47

SERVES 6

PREPARATION 20 min

COOKING 30 min

DIFFICULTY level 2

Cabbage Soup
with potatoes and bacon

Sauté the bacon in a large saucepan over medium heat until the fat has melted, about 5 minutes. • Stir in the butter and onion and sauté until the onion is softened, about 5 minutes. • Add the potato, 1/4 teaspoon of the paprika, and the marjoram. Sauté over low heat until the potato has almost softened, 8–10 minutes. • Keep stirring the mixture. Add the cabbage and pour in the water. Bring to a boil and simmer for 4–8 minutes, depending on how finely the cabbage was shredded—it should retain some crispness. Season with salt and pepper. • Stir in the sour cream, and add the sausage, if using. Return to a gentle boil. • Garnish with the parsley and dust with the remaining paprika. • Serve hot.

8 oz (250 g) bacon, chopped
1 teaspoon butter
1 large onion, finely chopped
1 large waxy potato, cut into small cubes
1 teaspoon sweet paprika
1 tablespoon finely chopped fresh marjoram or dill
1 green or Savoy cabbage, weighing about 1 1/2 lb (750 g), finely shredded
6 cups (1.5 liters) water
Salt and freshly ground white pepper
2/3 cup (150 ml) sour cream
4 oz (125 g) spicy, smoked sausage, thinly sliced (optional)
2 tablespoons finely chopped parsley

SERVES 4–6

PREPARATION 15 min

COOKING 1 h 15 min

DIFFICULTY level 1

Chicken Soup
with corn

Place the chicken in a large saucepan with the water, onion, celery, salt, and pepper. Bring to a boil over medium heat. Simmer over low heat until the chicken is tender, about 1 hour. • Remove the pan from the heat. Take the chicken out of the pot. Remove all the bones, skin, and any fat that has accumulated. Cut the chicken meat into rough pieces. • Return the vegetables and half the cooking liquid to the pan and blend with a handheld blender until almost smooth. • Return the chicken to the soup. Stir in the corn, creamed corn, and celery soup. Simmer over low heat, stirring constantly, for 10 minutes. • Remove from the heat and stir in the cream. • Garnish with the chives and serve hot.

1 small chicken, about 2 lb (1 kg), cut into 8 pieces
4 cups (1 liter) water
1 large onion, finely chopped
2 stalks celery, finely chopped
2 teaspoons salt
1 teaspoon freshly ground white pepper
1 (14-oz/400 g) can creamed corn (sweet corn)
1 (14-oz/400-g) can cream of celery soup
1/2 cup (125 ml) light (single) cream
Handful of chives, snipped, to garnish

Vegetable Cream

Heat the butter in a large saucepan over medium heat. Add the onion, celery, carrot, red pepper flakes, and caraway seeds and sauté until the vegetables are softened, about 10 minutes. • Add the bay leaf, parsley, garlic, dill, and cabbage. Sauté until the cabbage is wilted and half its original bulk, about 5 minutes. • Add the potatoes, turnips, salt, pepper, and stock. Bring to a boil, cover, and simmer for 30 minutes. • Add the tomatoes. Partially cover the pan and simmer on low heat for 30 minutes. • Discard the bay leaf. Purée the soup in a blender in two batches until free of lumps, but still with a bit of texture. Taste for salt and pepper. • Serve hot with a dollop of sour cream and a sprig of fresh dill.

2 tablespoons butter
1 large onion, chopped
2 large stalks celery, chopped
1 large carrot, chopped
Pinch of red pepper flakes
1 teaspoon caraway seeds
1 bay leaf
2 tablespoons finely chopped parsley
3 cloves garlic, finely chopped
Handful of chopped fresh dill
1 lb (500 g) cabbage, chopped
2 lb (1 kg) potatoes, peeled and cut into cubes
1 lb (500 g) turnips, peeled and coarsely chopped
1 teaspoon salt
1 teaspoon freshly ground black pepper
6 cups (1.5 liters) beef stock (homemade – see page 9 or bouillon cube)
1 (14-oz/400-g) can tomatoes, with juice
Sour cream, to garnish
A few sprigs of fresh dill, to garnish

SERVES 6–8

PREPARATION 30 min

COOKING 2 h

DIFFICULTY level 1

Beef Soup
with rice and spinach

Heat 4 tablespoons of the oil in a large saucepan over medium heat. Add the onions, garlic, and carrot and sauté until lightly browned, 8–10 minutes. • Add the beef and sauté until well browned, 8–10 minutes. • Add the water and tomatoes. Lower the heat, cover, and cook over low heat until the beef is tender, 90 minutes. • Stir in the rice and cook for 15 minutes. Add the spinach and cinnamon. Season with salt and pepper. Simmer for 10 minutes more. • Add the parsley and drizzle with remaining oil just before serving.

1/3 cup (90 ml) extra-virgin olive oil
2 onions, finely chopped
4 cloves garlic, finely chopped
1 small carrot, sliced
1 1/2 lb (750 g) stewing beef, cut into small chunks
12 cups (3 liters) cold water
2 tomatoes, chopped
3/4 cup (150 g) long-grain rice
2 lb (1 kg) fresh spinach, tough stems removed, or 1 lb (500 g) frozen spinach
1 teaspoon ground cinnamon
Salt and freshly ground black pepper
6 tablespoons finely chopped parsley

SERVES 4–6

PREPARATION 15 min

COOKING 30 min

DIFFICULTY level 1

Spicy Beef Soup
with potatoes

Heat the oil in a large soup pot over medium-high heat. Add the onion, garlic, carrot, celery, chile, and parsley and sauté until the onion is softened, about 5 minutes. • Add the beef and sauté until nicely browned, 5–7 minutes. • Add the tomatoes, potatoes, stock, salt, and pepper. Partially cover the pan and simmer over medium-low heat until the potatoes are tender, 15–20 minutes. • Garnish with the cilantro, if desired, and serve hot.

2 tablespoons extra-virgin olive oil

1 large white onion, finely chopped

2 cloves garlic, finely chopped

1 carrot, finely chopped

1 stalk celery, finely chopped

1 fresh red chile pepper, finely sliced

2 tablespoons finely chopped parsley

12 oz (350 g) ground (minced) beef

2 (14-oz/400-g) cans tomatoes, chopped, with juice

2–3 large potatoes, peeled and diced

4 cups (1 liter) beef stock (homemade — see page 9 or bouillon cube)

Salt and freshly ground black pepper

2 tablespoons finely chopped cilantro (coriander), to garnish, optional

Spanish Soup

with chorizo sausage and pork

Heat the oil in a large soup pot over medium heat. Add the onions and garlic and season with salt. Sauté until the onions are softened, about 5 minutes. • Stir in the paprika, chorizo, and pork. Sauté in the paprika mixture until lightly browned, 6–8 minutes. • Add the potatoes, bell peppers, beans, and tomatoes. Season with salt. Pour in the water and add the bay leaves and sage. Bring to a boil. Simmer over low heat until the vegetables are tender, about 45 minutes. • Season with salt and pepper to taste. Remove the bay leaves. Stir in the parsley. • Serve hot.

$1/3$ cup (90 ml) extra-virgin olive oil

2 large Spanish onions, finely chopped

4 cloves garlic, finely chopped

Salt

$1\frac{1}{2}$ teaspoons sweet paprika

8 oz (250 g) chorizo sausage, sliced

8 oz (250 g) roasted pork loin,
    cut into cubes

2 potatoes, peeled and cut in small cubes

1 red bell pepper (capsicum),
    seeded and diced

1 green bell pepper (capsicum),
    seeded and diced

1 (14-oz/400-g) can garbanzo beans
    (chickpeas), drained

6–8 tomatoes, peeled and chopped

6 cups (1.5 liters) cold water

2 bay leaves

2 teaspoons finely chopped sage

Freshly ground black pepper

3 tablespoons finely chopped parsley

Minestrone
with sausage and pancetta

Heat the oil in a large soup pot over medium heat. Add the onion and sauté until softened, about 5 minutes. • Add the pancetta, potato, and carrot and cook for 5 minutes. Add the split peas, stock, and marjoram and bring to a boil. Boil for 2 minutes, skimming off any froth. Partially cover and simmer until the soup has thickened and the peas have softened, about 45 minutes. • Remove the pancetta from the soup, trim off any fat, and cut into small cubes. Return the pancetta to the soup and stir in the sausage and parsley. • Reheat the soup and season with salt and pepper. Simmer for 5 minutes more. • Serve hot.

2 tablespoons extra-virgin olive oil

1 large onion, finely chopped

1 (8-oz/250-g) piece lean pancetta

1 potato, finely chopped

1 small carrot, finely chopped

2½ cups (250 g) green split peas

6 cups (1.5 liters) chicken stock (homemade or bouillon cube)

½ teaspoon dried marjoram

Salt and freshly ground black pepper

4 oz (125 g) German ham sausage, cut into small cubes

1 tablespoon finely chopped parsley

SERVES 6–8

PREPARATION 45 min

COOKING 1 h

DIFFICULTY level 2

Chestnut Soup
with squash and ginger

Melt the butter with the oil in a large, heavy saucepan over medium heat. Add the onion, carrot, celery, and red pepper flakes. Sauté until the onion is softened, about 5 minutes. • Add the garlic, ginger, squash, sweet potatoes, potatoes, sea salt, stock, and chopped chestnuts. There should be enough stock to cover the vegetables and for the vegetables to move about easily when stirred. If not, add more stock or water. Bring to a boil, then cover and simmer over very low heat for 1 hour, stirring occasionally. Add more stock or water if the soup becomes too thick or begins to stick to the bottom of the pan. The squash and potatoes should fall apart when pierced with a fork. • Purée the soup in two batches in a blender. Taste for salt and pepper. • Serve hot with a drizzle of oil and sprinkled with the chives.

1 tablespoon butter

2 tablespoons extra-virgin olive oil

1 medium yellow onion, chopped

1 carrot, chopped

1 celery stalk, chopped

1/8 teaspoon crushed red pepper flakes

3 cloves garlic, finely chopped

2 tablespoons minced fresh ginger

1 3/4 lb (800 g) squash or pumpkin, peeled and cut into small cubes

12 oz (350 g) sweet potatoes, peeled and cut into small cubes

2 medium potatoes, peeled and cut into small cubes

1 teaspoon coarse sea salt

4 cups (1 liter) beef stock + more as required (homemade — see page 9 — or bouillon cube)

1 lb (500 g) chestnuts, roasted, peeled, and chopped

Salt and freshly ground black pepper

Extra-virgin olive oil and fresh chives, to garnish

Garbanzo Soup
with mushrooms

Put the garbanzo beans in a medium saucepan with water to cover. Bring to a boil over medium heat. Cover and simmer until tender, about 90 minutes. Drain reserving the cooking liquid. • Heat half the oil in a large saucepan over medium heat. Add the garlic and rosemary and sauté until pale golden brown, 2–3 minutes. • Add the dried mushrooms, button mushrooms, and potatoes. Season with salt and pepper. Add a ladle of the reserved cooking liquid and mix well. • Simmer for 10 minutes. Add the garbanzo beans and half the remaining cooking liquid. Cover and simmer until the vegetables are very tender, about 15 minutes. • Ladle into soup bowls and sprinkle with parsley. Drizzle with the remaining oil. • Serve with hot with the toast.

1½ cups (150 g) dried garbanzo beans (chickpeas), soaked overnight and drained

⅓ cup (90 ml) extra-virgin olive oil

1 clove garlic, finely chopped

1 tablespoon finely chopped rosemary

1 oz (30 g) dried mushrooms, soaked in warm water for 15 minutes, drained, and chopped

1 lb (500 g) button mushrooms, sliced

2 small potatoes, peeled and cut into small cubes

Salt and freshly ground black pepper

1 tablespoon finely chopped parsley

8 slices warm toasted whole-wheat (wholemeal) bread

Vegetable Soup
with beans and fresh herbs

Heat the oil in a large saucepan over medium heat. Add the onion, garlic, and leek. Sauté until softened, about 5 minutes. • Add the basil, parsley, thyme, marjoram, and sage. Sauté for 10 minutes. • Add the tomatoes and simmer over low heat until they have broken down, about 10 minutes. • Add the zucchini, potatoes, turnip, carrots, green beans, kidney beans, water, and spinach. Season with salt and pepper. Bring to a boil then simmer over low heat until the vegetables are very tender, about 1 hour. • Serve hot.

3 tablespoons extra-virgin olive oil
1 large onion, finely chopped
2 cloves garlic, finely chopped
1 leek, sliced
2 tablespoons finely chopped basil
2 tablespoons finely chopped parsley
1 tablespoon finely chopped thyme
1 tablespoon finely chopped marjoram
$\frac{1}{2}$ tablespoon finely chopped sage
4 tomatoes, peeled and chopped
4 medium zucchini (courgettes), chopped
3 potatoes, peeled and cut in small cubes
2 small turnips, peeled and chopped
3 large carrots, peeled and chopped
7 oz (200 g) green beans, chopped
1 cup (250 g) canned white kidney beans
8 cups (2 liters) boiling water
8 oz (250 g) fresh spinach, shredded
Salt and freshly ground black pepper

SERVES 4–6

PREPARATION 15 min

COOKING 1 h 30 min

DIFFICULTY level 1

Vegetable Soup
with rice and cabbage

Place the water in a large saucepan over medium heat. Add the onion, potatoes, celery, carrots, zucchini, beans, and tomatoes. Mix well and bring to a boil. Season with salt and pepper. Partially cover the pan and simmer over low heat until the vegetables are very tender, about 1 hour. Add a little more water if required. • Stir in the tomato paste, cabbage, and peas. Cook for 10 minutes. • Add the rice. and simmer until tender, 10–15 minutes. Remove from the heat and let rest for 5 minutes. • Add a little more pepper and mix well. Sprinkle with the Parmesan and serve hot.

8 cups (2 liters) water + more as required

1 large onion, finely chopped

2 large potatoes, peeled and cut into small cubes

2 celery sticks, finely chopped

2 large carrots, sliced

3 medium zucchini (courgettes), chopped

5 oz (150 g) canned red kidney or borlotti beans

2 large ripe tomatoes, peeled and chopped

Salt and freshly ground black pepper

1 tablespoon tomato paste (concentrate)

10 oz (300 g) savoy cabbage, shredded

1 cup (150 g) frozen peas

1/2 cup (100 g) long grain rice

1/4 cup (30 g) freshly grated Parmesan

60

Aduki Bean

soup

Heat the oil in a large saucepan over medium heat. Add the onions, celery, carrots, garlic, thyme, and bay leaves and sauté until the onion is softened, about 5 minutes. • Pour in the stock and add the aduki beans. Bring to a boil and simmer over low heat until the beans are tender, about 1 hour. • Stir in the tomatoes and tomato paste and simmer for 20 minutes. • Season with salt and pepper and stir in the parsley. Serve hot.

$1/4$ cup (60 ml) sunflower oil

2 onions, finely chopped

2 stalks celery, finely chopped

3 carrots, finely chopped

2 cloves garlic, finely chopped

1 (14-oz/400-g) can tomatoes, chopped, with juice

1 tablespoon tomato paste (concentrate)

1 tablespoon finely chopped thyme leaves, or 1 teaspoon dried thyme

2 bay leaves

7 cups (1.75 liters) chicken stock (homemade or bouillon cube)

$1^1/4$ cups (200 g) dried aduki beans, soaked overnight and drained

Salt and freshly ground black pepper

2 tablespoons finely chopped parsley

4 tablespoons freshly grated Cheddar or Emmenthal cheese, to serve

SERVES 4

PREPARATION 30 min + 2 h to chill

DIFFICULTY level 1

Cool Avocado
cream with fresh mint

Cut the avocados in half lengthwise and twist each half so that the large pit breaks free from the flesh. Peel the avocados. • Process the avocado flesh with the onion, garlic, cilantro, mint, lime juice, and 1½ cups (375 ml) of the stock in a food processor or blender until smooth. • Pour in the remaining stock, the rice vinegar, and soy sauce. Season with salt and pepper. • Cover with plastic wrap and chill in the refrigerator for at least 2 hours. • Garnish with lime zest and serve cold.

2 firm-ripe avocados
1 small onion, finely chopped
1 clove garlic, lightly crushed but whole
2 tablespoons finely chopped cilantro (coriander)
1 tablespoon finely chopped mint
2 tablespoons fresh lime juice
3 cups (750 ml) vegetable stock (homemade or bouillon cube)
1 tablespoon rice vinegar
1 tablespoon light soy sauce
Salt and freshly ground black pepper
Shredded lime zest, to garnish